Towards ballet

Towards ballet
Dance training for the very young

Beryl F. Manthorp

DANCE BOOKS   CECIL COURT LONDON

First published by Dance Books Ltd., 9 Cecil Court,
London WC2N 4EZ, in 1980. This edition published 1988.
© 1980, 1988 Beryl F. Manthorp
British Library Cataloguing in Publication Data
Manthorp, Beryl F.
 Towards Ballet: dance training for the very young.
 1. Ballet dancing—Study and teaching
 2. Dancing—Children's dances
 I. Title
 792.8'2'07   GV1788.5
 ISBN 1-85273-006-4

Frontispiece: Left, a baby three years old—right, pre-primary nearly five years

Contents

Dedication

To the girls who suffered my baby class and later brought their own children. My thanks to the first generation who taught me much that I hope will be a help to the second.

Introduction

Two-and-a-half to five years is an age range rarely taught by professional dance teachers organisations. Those classes shown have been demonstrations, with little explanation or discussion on the method, the thought behind the activities, or the ultimate dance movements developed from baby "games."

The "whys and wherefores" at this stage are very important. The teacher must know where she is leading her pupils.

The idea for this book grew from a lecture demonstration, given at a day course. It is based on long years of teaching babies and, I hope, may be of some help to young teachers and students.

It seems presumptuous to state my own methods. These are intended as examples. Only by having someone else's ideas in the first place can one invent and develop one's own, with experience, according to the needs of the class.

Acknowledgements

I owe a big 'thank you' to many people who have helped me to produce this book.

Firstly to Peter Brinson for his constant interest, practical help and valuable advice throughout all stages.

To Mrs Patricia M Mackenzie, BA, ARAD, Senior Lecturer in Charge of Ballet Studies, Laban Art of Movement Centre, Goldsmiths' College, University of London, and Mrs Betty Hassall, ARAD, Adv. Teacher's Cert. LISTD (CB), Children's examiner of The Royal Academy of Dancing; Principal, the Hammond School, Chester, both of whom gave their time to read the typescript so thoroughly and gave valuable suggestions from their experience in training teachers.

To John Field, CBE, ARAD, for his interest and for reading the notes on which the book is based.

To Frank Freeman for encouragement and belief that this would be of real help to students, young teachers and those unaccustomed to pupils of this age.

To Mrs Winifred Fowles who has played for my baby classes for many years, invented musical accompaniment to fit my exercises and improvisations to my instant ideas at the drop of a hat. Also for typing the manuscript from my handwriting which varies from hour to hour.

To the parents and children and to Elizabeth King for patience and time spent posing for photographs and to Edgar Spelman for taking these.

To the young teachers of the East Anglian region of the Royal Academy of Dancing who first asked for my help in teaching their very young pupils, and for whom the original notes were assembled.

To Michele Neave for being such a good student who was at first scared of the babies. It was for Michele that the notes were reassembled and elaborated for future reference.

To all my baby classes throughout the years who have taught me so much.

None of the children whose photographs appear in this book had reached their fifth birthday when the photographs were taken.

Photographs by Edgar C. Spelman, Norwich.

Foreword

Forewords are a problem. If an author has done her job well, why need one? Beryl Manthorp seems to me to have done her job excellently in two ways. First, she has discerned a gap in the provision of literature about dance for very young children. There really is nothing to match what she has written, so this book fills a real need. Second, she writes out of profound personal experience and knowledge, being one of our most distinguished experts on the subject. Chairman of the East Anglian region of the Royal Academy of Dancing of which she is a life member, founder and director of one of the best-known private dance studios in her part of England, lecturer on the teaching of young children to the Royal Academy of Dancing, Beryl Manthorp has been guide and teacher to generations of dance students and their parents as she leads many of them from baby class through the grades into professional examinations. She is not exclusively a baby's teacher. Nor does she talk readily about her achievements, so this at least is something a foreword can do usefully. I've known Beryl Manthorp, and watched her work, for more than a decade, first, briefly, when I was Director of the Royal Academy of Dancing, then as colleague in many dance ventures from the growth of *Ballet for All*, to teaching occasions in East Anglia, to performances of her own school planned and presented meticulously, to our most recent collaboration when she has been a valued member of the Gulbenkian Action Conference on Dance Education.

Inevitably writers reflect much of themselves in their books and the reflection illuminates what we know of them even though this reflection is usually unconscious. Another job for a foreword, therefore, is to indicate the reflections. Beryl Manthorp's book reveals especially her unspoken approach to teaching, the things she takes for granted. One of them is her insistence on good music and its link with dance. This comes through in her writing, but is so fundamental to good dance teaching it needs emphasising first. Next is her sympathy for children *and* parents. Too often for teachers parents are a chore. The children sense this and conflicts build up. You won't find such attitudes in this book. Another link is between theatre and classroom. I *don't* mean that her babies are trained for theatre careers I *do* mean she encourages them to express themselves and dance their own thing within the context of her teaching, a doing which reaches its climax every other year in the school show. Classical ballet is supposed to be only for those who are specially gifted, even at an age when gifts can hardly have begun to show. This really isn't true. Dancing is indivisible. The teacher is decisive, and in Beryl Manthorp's book this is the most important reflection of all.

Peter Brinson
Director, UK and Commonwealth Branch, Calouste Gulbenkian Foundation, Chairman, Dance Board, Council for National Academic Awards.

Part one

The approach to the teaching of babies

Chapter 1   Pupils and teachers

Small children are not undersized adults, nor are they an unintelligent mass, nor even are they future dancers. They are easily influenced—mentally and physically pliable. Their ability to express themselves never equals their comprehension. At two-and-a-half years of age they have usually grown to half their final height but they have relatively large heads and short arms. They vary very much in rate of growth, dexterity, brain power, clarity of speech and family background.

Small children are people—individuals who will one day have a say in the world but, as yet, lack knowledge and experience. It is the duty of all of us who come into contact with children to see that we impart this knowledge and provide this experience. As dance teachers we should do this with an emphasis towards music and movement.

Often it is advisable and indeed necessary to allow children to find things out for themselves. However, a teacher cannot always do this in the same way as a parent. With several children to control at the same time discipline must be observed. If a child injures itself in class it will be the teacher's fault, at least most parents will think so. The fact that the school is insured does not compensate for the effect on all concerned. It is not only a wise precaution, but essential to remove every article of potential danger such as scissors. It is preferable to have an all but empty hall or studio with the piano and possibly a few stable chairs. Keys, locks, bolts and fasteners of all kinds have a fascination for children and as far as possible must be kept out of reach.

Discipline must be enforced quietly, gently but firmly. Correction must fit the situation and be administered immediately. Children will not resent this, but will come to respect the teacher (although parents will sometimes consider the teacher unnecessarily strict).

For many years I was a visiting teacher at a private boarding school for boys and girls up to the age of eleven. The headmistress, a trained and experienced teacher, was also a brilliant musician and played for my classes. I reaped the benefits of this not only for her beautiful accompaniment, but also by watching her handling her pupils. A strict disciplinarian who never tired of correcting her children, she had no favourites, but had a tremendous sense of humour and she loved them all and they adored her. Her pupils learned something for life in everything they did, their training was "comprehensive" in a quite different sense from what this term has come to mean today. Dancing was a natural and necessary part of education for all girls—not an optional extra subject. After her retirement, all the boys also took dance classes—the new headmaster took the view that dancing was not a purely feminine activity.

Baby classes can be most educational for all small boys and girls. The fact that infants are easily influenced and copy adults puts a great responsibility on the teacher's shoulders—something never to be forgotten. Deportment, manners and speech become mirrored in little people. Woe betide the teacher who has several mannerisms.

Physically, the baby group should be able to perform a great number of movements but technique should be handled with care, especially any jumps. Children either "walk or talk." Those who do not move well and have poor balance can often carry on a most lucid conversation with clarity of speech and vice-versa. This does not mean that those who never utter a word, or whose chatter is quite unintelligible do not understand just as well. Adults with no connection or experience of tiny children often ask if my baby class understands me.

Concentration is, of course, lacking in all very young children, but their attitude and ability to learn often reflects their home background. For example: the youngest child in a large family will usually be advanced for his or her years; an only child may be apprehensive of other members of the class; one whose parents rarely read or talk to their children may be at a loss to follow the lesson. Always ask for the date of birth, because the size of a child can be very misleading. Three months difference can be quite a gap and six months is a separate age group.

Teachers should never leave the room during baby class, the children would be out of hand when returning to "pick up the reins". Always keep the lesson non-stop—ie the teacher must be prepared to talk all the time thus avoiding "losing" the class, especially between activities, when re-organisation takes place.

Children should be encouraged to do things for themselves. Often this means waiting for something an adult could do in half the time. Children love to help. In class they can take turns in fetching the register and pen, another two children will then return these to a safe place. Replacing "props" should be carried out by the pupils if possible.

Children are unkind to each other, some more than others. Generally they dislike being left out of a group. But those who refuse to join in learn a great deal by watching, and often surprise parents by demonstrating some movements at home. During the period between two-and-a-half and four-and-a-half years a great deal is learnt that will never be forgotten, but the pupil will not remember being taught.

Students and young teachers should be prepared for awkward questions, as even they are often thought of as old. For example "Can you take your teeth out, my granny can!"

Chapter 2   Education through dance

1   From a teacher's point of view, of what should a baby class consist?
Careful instruction through music and movement, designed to benefit every child, and which they will enjoy.

Children between two-and-a-half and four years learn quickly and understand more than most adults seem to think. Possibly 99.9 per cent of the children in baby class will never be dancers, but they should all benefit from the class.

2   To what precise benefits should the instruction be directed?
Enjoyment, mixing and working with others, listening and moving to music, obedience, confidence, ability to move and feel all parts of the body, learning to concentrate and to take one's place in a group—learning to learn.

Perhaps I have not put these in the best order, but that is not of great importance. What does matter is that these classes do play a part in forming personalities—what has been called "making people." Any teacher has an influence over her pupils.

3   A baby class should never be:
Too long. Children of this age have to be encouraged to concentrate. Up to an hour and no longer is the best time to be allowed, and this is only possible if the teacher has planned the class in advance to give it variety. As soon as attention flags that particular activity should be changed to another. As explained later, one exercise should be contrasted with the next—ie a quiet, sitting exercise be followed by one requiring more lively movement. One important fact teachers have to remember is that baby class often has "to be played by ear."

A disorganised run-about. A means of passing time when mother can be relieved of the child for a while, a haphazard arrangement of activities, or a lesson in technique. Baby class should begin on the right road. "Success or failure in all studies depends chiefly on the manner in which they are commenced" (*The Code of Terpsichore*, Carlos Blasis, London 1830).

4   What do you teach babies?
A question I find difficult to answer to the uninitiated. The class is based on stories and ideas suitable to the age group, using actions representing natural or inanimate objects with which the children can identify and have an opportunity to observe. Class activities should aim at increasing knowledge of its "themes" as well as developing an awareness of a pupil's own body and its

capabilities as well as providing a foundation for the basic technique of any school of movement.

The human body is limited to two legs, feet, arms and hands with one torso and head, therefore it is restricted in the variety of movements possible in any form of physical activity no matter in which style, technique, pattern or expression it is performed. For example, there are only five jumps: from two feet to two feet, from two feet to one foot, from one foot to two feet, from one foot to the other, from one foot landing on the same foot. Whatever style, technique, pattern or expression is used, there are no other ways of jumping.

However, I do not believe these classes should be unstructured, haphazard or unrelated from lesson to lesson. A system of progression with variety must be maintained to avoid boredom and overstrain in any part of the body. A structured, systematic preparation of every lesson provides satisfaction for the children, particularly when a certain stage has been reached or movement mastered. This leads to understanding and appreciation from the parents with the knowledge that time and money have not been wasted.

Programmes of activities for the very young baby class vary very little from week to week. At this age children gain confidence and a sense of security from the familiar. They always want the same bedtime story, even though they know it by heart. Because of this it is imperative that the arrangement of the class covers all aspects of the training, and yet does not overtire the children or become dull.

5   General knowledge

Educationalists criticise most dancing lessons as not being of educational value, as they only teach children steps and insist pupils are "taught" dancing and not taught "through" dancing. This is possibly true in many cases. However it need not be and should not be in the hands of a good teacher.

General knowledge in baby class is included in a variety of ways, for example—

Counting   How many toes? when learning to place the feet correctly. How many fingers? Use the hands. Four fingers and one thumb makes five; One foot and one foot makes two feet. Older classes can dance skips for eight, wait for eight or clap eight. Two sets of eight together make sixteen. Teachers should not use more than two sets for children of this age group because too many variations will be confusing.

Days of the week   Can be brought into class by asking what day it is, what will tomorrow be etc. Older classes can mime actions associated with special days.

Reminders   To keep to the path when travelling round the room or making patterns.

Right and left   These can be learnt with hands and feet, though this should not be attempted with the very young baby class.

Colours   This is very easy to include when having children a few at a time, the "blue dresses," the "white socks" groups for example. When using props try to match the colours with the dresses. For older babies "painting" colours according to the tone of the music.

Observation   Characterisations from nature are suitable, ie butterflies and how they fly and fold their wings upwards. Tulips—how they grow to a point before opening and petals fall one by one. Daisies (small, wild ones)—only grow a little way, open out looking at the sky and close up at night.

Vocabulary   This can be increased by introducing the correct termi-nology. When encouraging babies to "dance" with their heads and eyes, we "incline" our heads. By demonstrating herself the teacher can show the meaning of the word and the children will delight in repeating it when asked. Never confuse the class with too many words, but remember to repeat the ones used for several weeks.

Music   Accent, rhythm, pitch, speed and volume should be included in baby class activities. By "using" the phrase, shape and feeling of the music as well the children will be encouraged to listen and hear the music. Once mastered this is never lost. In school life the training gained in baby class will be a joy to the music staff as well as to the dance teacher. However the sense of rhythm will be there for a future working life, maybe for a typist for example. Sports will also benefit from early rhythm training, for instance skating, gymnastics, tennis, and riding, because a correct rhythmic approach is essential in most activities if they are to be successful.

The social graces   By tradition these are linked with dancing: "Good breeding demands that pleasing and easy manner which can only be gained by dancing" (Pierre Rameau, *The Dancing Master*, Paris 1725).

   Manners, whether good or bad are a habit. Good manners are taught by example to the very young. In class the pianist should be "involved" not just an accompanist. The children should recognise and appreciate the pianist—if it is at all possible, take them to speak to him or her and suggest a "thank you for playing." Similarly each child should shake hands with the teacher and say "goodbye" at the end of every class.

Physical skills   These are helped by dance classes. As well as movements such as run, jump, walk etc strength and control of hands for writing, drawing or playing some instrument can be gained; balance and coordination, especially of that between eyes and hands are of particular value.

Through baby class knowledge will be acquired and experience gained, none of which is a waste, whether the pupil is to be a dancer, an enthusiastic onlooker or just a member of the public.

Chapter 3   Parents and pianists

Teacher and pupils must be the principal characters in a baby class, but parents and pianists also have a role. In nine cases out of ten even little tots are better without parents watching, although I like mothers to stay for the first and maybe a few subsequent classes. That is until the pupil has confidence, especially if this is the child's first experience of being taught by a stranger. Once confidence has been established, I do not mind if parents watch or not. Children's reactions are very different. Some want mother all the time, some refuse to join in or become naughty if mother is there. Others are not bothered in any way. At times a mother will join in to help a shy child. I suspect these mothers to be parents who had learnt dancing themselves. Some mothers are just as shy as their baby, so do not have the courage to get "involved."

One of my grumbles about adults watching is their chatter and another the noise they allow to be made by the pupil's brothers and sisters who are sometimes brought along to watch. Adults forget how a child's attention wanders, particularly if they hear their own mother's voice and perhaps their own name. Parents also fail to realise how much harder the teacher's task becomes working against a constant babble. Quite often I have to ask my audience to refrain from talking more than once in a single class.

Not all mothers are insensitive to the need for quiet: many are very interested in their little one's lesson and will practice with them at home, giving reminders from the last class. The really keen parent will learn with the child. When going through my notes for this book I realised how much baby class depends on the parent and how little I really knew as to why they brought their children in the first place.

Finally I drew up a questionnaire to help me understand their point of view, their opinions of the work and its effect on their particular child. A summary of my findings reveals a very wide variety of reasons for sending the child to baby class. Among these were: to learn dancing and music; to learn movement; to mix with other children; to build confidence; because the child saw dancing on TV and wanted to copy; because she was always falling over through not looking where she was going, she was now much better; because she has two brothers and this is a girlie activity.

Technique is not a part of baby class so I listed the possible benefits which might be derived by young children attending these classes and asked their parents to tick the list of elements in which they felt their own child had made progress. The majority found the child had gained in coordination, confidence and discipline, and many that deportment and concentration were improved. Others mentioned greater dexterity and ability to mix with others as well as observation. Very few felt their child had gained speed in learning.

The role of the pianist will be developed later, she is such an important part of the class. It is only right that this point should be acknowledged and understood before discussing the musical accompaniment required for exercises and activities.

Like the teacher, the pianist is affected by too much noise and distraction. If unable to hear the teacher clearly, it is impossible for her to be at her best. The ideal form of accompaniment is improvisation: a musician who cannot improvise is not really suitable for baby class. The pianist needs to understand the approach to the class, the object of each activity, to be the teacher's partner and the children's friend.

Chapter 4   Ideals and preparation

The ideal class is almost an impossibility, but ideals we must have. The teacher has a responsibility to the children and to the parents. A good baby class gives a sound foundation for dance training. It takes away some of the drudgery as so much knowledge and basic ability will have been assimilated without the pupil noticing the fact. Though 99 per cent of the children will not be dancers, the lessons will never be a waste and remain with the pupils for life. Unfortunately the educational value of dance classes for the very young children is not always recognised.

Movement without rhythm, balance, bend, stretch, arm movements and without the use of head and eyes in some form or other I do not call dance. Each of these must be started immediately. Elevation, turns, use of arms and hands, transfer of weight are all begun in the babies' first lesson disguised in ways they can follow and enjoy. Feet, legs, body, arms, hands, head and eyes all have their individual exercises from the beginning. As time progresses coordination is introduced.

Though what is taught should be much the same as would be given to older beginners, the most important points for this age group are: listening to the music, being able to feel and move all parts of the body and performing expressive movements and stories. The latter, if kept up as children get older, helps to make less self-conscious performers and produces the communication between dancer and dancer, as well as dancer and the audience.

To feel movement can be fun at two-and-a-half to four years and is needed to facilitate the correction of faults later on. As already mentioned (see p. 15) expressive movements, presented as games, can be of educational value both physically and mentally.

Preparing a class needs careful thought. The following six points should be taken into consideration:

1   **The class must be interesting.**   Interest is provided by stories, variety of activities and musical expression.
2   **The class must have technical variety.**   This must include several sitting-down exercises. Feet exercises sitting still tire tiny legs, so give some other activity before standing up.
3   **The class must not overtire,** either the whole child nor any one part of the body.
4   **The class must bear repeating.**   As small children like familiarity and repetition, for two- to three-and-a-half-year-olds the same basic class every week is ideal, so the plan must include everything to be taught in a variety of ways.

5 The class must be adaptable. The necessity to improvise often occurs. The order or patter may have to be changed to fit the day's happenings or conditions. But with practice the teacher can steer the class on the chosen course.

6 The class must be geared for progression. The simplest way of doing any exercise is essential at the beginning but the teacher must have progressions in mind in order to increase the standard while still maintaining the familiar.

From two to five years of age is a time when children learn an enormous amount, when they form the habit of learning, *and when they want to learn.*

When discussing the preparation of class I must include music and props. "Be prepared" should be the motto. A good pianist, who normally improvises, can be taken ill suddenly, or be prevented from playing for a few weeks. A new pianist may need practical guidance for a while. It might never be possible to get a good "baby" pianist at the right time of the week.

One suitable form of accompaniment is a book of nursery rhymes. An album with a good number, not just the well-known ones, could be used as a last resort. There are many books of musical exercises or excerpts from longer works arranged for movement accompaniment. These usually include a selection of different time signatures. Once the actual music is at hand, a pianist should be able to change it into any rhythm or expression (see appendix). Many very good pianists cannot improvise a note without some music. Avoid difficult and tuneless music—it does not help the children. Always have the nursery rhymes ready.

I always have my "emergency tape" that is a tape especially recorded for baby class work should I find myself without a pianist at any time. This tape can be pressed into use, but it is necessary to have a second person to operate the machine. With babies the teacher must be "with the class," not keep running away to stop or restart a tape. "No pianist" is a real calamity, but if the class cannot be stopped in time, or an alternative pianist engaged, the teacher cannot send the children away. Some form of percussion, drums, tambour, tambourine could be more successful than a tape as the teacher could "play" as she demonstrates the movements.

Props I use dolls, teddies etc, which the children bring themselves. A favourite toy will help a child to feel at home and be a great help in some activities. Balls, not too small or too large also have great value to training. Most children want to "play ball," just a few are nervous.

Coloured sashes or bands (Such as used for identification in team games.) I use them for marking circles and lines on the floor, as well as to link the children in "trains." The balls and bands, or any other small prop the teacher wishes to use should be handy, but out of reach until needed.

Chapter 5   Teacher's approach

Before describing the movements I use, a few words are needed about the teacher's own technique in handling the class, controlling the children and putting over her material.

I prefer not to be in the studio before the time to start the lesson, but remain within earshot in case of emergency. There are always plenty of odd jobs to keep me occupied right up to the last minute, but the main reason is that my arrival draws the attention of the children.

The teacher should enter the room, put down any equipment she might be carrying and with bright "good afternoon" or "good morning," whichever is applicable, *get started* before the children's attention wanders. Begin the class on time: this is a part of class discipline, and the teacher should show herself a disciplined person. Close the door. Little children can slip out with alarming speed. Once the class has started the teacher is responsible and some parents will have gone away. The handle of my studio door is too high for the babies to open by themselves, and this I find a great comfort. Any messages or announcements for the grownups in charge of the children should be left until the end of class. Quite often these adults will not be the children's own parents. Families join together, taking it in turns to bring the children. Then there are Nannies, Grandparents, Aunts and just friends. It is essential to emphasise messages, when they have to be passed on.

Always choose the first activity carefully, remembering latecomers. Never make it difficult for an extra child to join in; something static or a circle is best.

The circle method should not be tried with the two-and-a-half- to three-and-a-half-years set. Small children may refuse to hold hands with each other, though keen to hold the teacher's hand. They have sharp little nails and may pinch or squeeze their partner or neighbour until it hurts. When first joining the really tinies into a circle I use their "dolls" to "join hands" between each child. This takes time to organise, so is unsuitable to start class.

The physical effort required from the class should be geared towards the weakest. Individual children cannot be set slightly different exercises according to their standard of development as can be done in older classes. I have often read articles on young children's ability which I think underestimates the average child. Such things as—"By the age of five they should be able to bounce a large ball." Many three-year-olds can bounce and catch a small ball. When a child refuses to join in with any special activity, the reason may be very hard to find. The use of balls will entice nearly every child from the perimeter of the class.

However, a watch must be kept so as not to overwork the young pupils. Try for a balance of physical and mental effort. Tiny children find slow movements very difficult. "Fairies" are always more rhythmical than "giants." The balance and control needed for slow movements comes from mental ability; one can note that the child who is bright and mentally advanced for his age can be more in time than the "little dancer." Of course those with real balance problems will find controlled standing movements difficult for a long time.

A constant battle in class is to get the children to spread out so that both they and the teacher have room to move. In the youngest group there is no point in striving for this, but later "bands" can be used as doorsteps, houses, rings, roadways etc, to encourage the use of space. Even with this method they will pick up their bands and move as close as possible to another member of the class. Therefore the teacher has to be quietly persistent.

It has been said that the baby class copy the teacher, but they will also copy each other. If a child behaves in an odd manner, distract his or her attention from this behaviour by calling attention to something else. *Never* point out the oddity. This is the quickest way to get the whole class behaving in the same way.

Visiting the toilet is also catching. Once one starts the fashion most of the class will follow. In some studios this can be a problem and a distraction. If possible have a toilet where the little ones can go on their own. I have a small child's toilet handy in a lobby leading from the studio, quite a way from the entrance door. When a baby "disappears" it is no worry and passes almost unnoticed—usually. Even small girls get up to tricks and lock each other out. The door into the lobby has glass panels so I can see the victim (catching the culprit is more difficult). Whenever a teacher contemplates teaching very young classes the toilet problem should be borne in mind and suitable provisions made. A puddle on the floor cannot be helped sometimes. This should be dealt with without fuss, because the child will be very upset.

A good voice is a necessary part of any teacher's equipment but with the babies it is *very* important. Whether children enjoy the class or not can depend on the way in which each activity is presented. Never use a monotonous voice or too many repetitions of words. Try objective encouragement, eg "see if you can reach the ceiling." The teacher's voice can emphasise many musical qualities, eg "down and up"—"slow and quick" etc. Always think before speaking and never make statements which cannot be carried out. Teachers must be quick thinkers.

Take the babies seriously. Listen to their chatter. They can be very funny, but should never be laughed at. How I hate to see tots on a stage just being natural, making a mess of some simple dance arrangement and the audience roaring with laughter. Baby "news" must be attended to, even though it takes time. Teachers amass an enormous amount of completely useless information

Just a conversation piece

about Daddy's new socks, Mummy's birthday and frills on petticoats etc. Conversation with children can be enlightening and humorous.

Before leaving the subject of teacher's technique, I would like to mention something about a teacher's own demonstration in class, which should always be good. Children copy faults with the greatest of ease. It is necessary to perform nearly everything with the class. Watch the effect of this and learn by mistakes. For example: if too much turn-out is used the babies will "sickle" when pointing their feet to the front. First position of the arms (RAD), when used, needs to be lower than normal, because the teacher is taller than the pupils her arms appear much higher and so little ones will therefore go up to shoulder level. I do not teach "arm positions" but these come in such exercises as picking flowers (see baby class page 42).

In the case of one or two troublesome infants in the class, deal with these, but at the same time try to keep the rest occupied. An idle baby class soon gets out of hand. One must be able to "make a point" if children misbehave and stick to one's word. I use "trains," the children's favourite game. We always leave this to the end of class. If behaviour has not been good it is omitted for some or all of the class. It works wonders!

Chapter 6   Exercises and activities with progressions

It has been stated that baby class could form the basis for any dance technique. This is my firm belief. Even the beauty of the upturned feet as seen in the dances of the Far East should benefit from "hello toes and goodbye toes." However, in the development of some exercises the reader may notice a trend towards ballet. This is my subject. The educational benefits of this style of dance are many and varied.

Ballet is a discipline which embraces all parts of the body and mind. It has direct links with music, painting, drama, literature, geography, history, anatomy and French. There is an end product, either as an amateur performer or knowledgeable onlooker or as a professional performer, teacher, writer, choreographer, notator or administrator. The physical training and general knowledge begun in baby class should be extended continually through training. Good deportment and carriage of the body will be an asset when setting foot on the lower rungs of the ladder leading to full adult life.

Class exercises

The progressions described below cover about one-and-a-half to two years of training (approximately two-and-a-half to four-and-a-half years of age). I group babies into three "grades." Even if one class follows the other and part of the time overlaps (as mostly happens in my school) I find this idea works. There is no hard and fast age limit for each group, but if children start at two-and-a-half years of age I would say approximately two-and-a-half to three-and-a-half years for the first two groups, and three-and-a-half to four-and-a-half years for the third. Some pupils pass quickly into the second grade, once they can behave well and skip—often these are younger sisters—then spend longer in the next class. Others, more uncoordinated and less disciplined, will need longer before being promoted. A rough guide to my use of the progressions listed would be:

> Exercises (a) in the first grade.
> Exercises (b) and (c) in the second grade.
> Exercises (d) and (e) in the third grade.

These are all very basic exercises, necessary for good movement, for example exercises 1 and 2 will be the foundation for jumps.

"When you bend to jump, the instep, by its strength, raises you in a lively manner" (Pierre Rameau, *The Dancing Master*).

The musical accompaniment should fit each movement exactly, with obvious marked rhythm (see Appendix). If notated music is to be used this should be marked beforehand, to avoid the pianist dithering and fumbling during the lesson as this makes it difficult for the teacher to maintain the children's interest. It also wastes time.

Advice to pianists   Avoid:
1   Music with too many chords or decorations.
2   Playing too long without a stop for exercises such as run, skip and walk; rabbits, dolls and butterflies also "trains." Babies' legs need a rest.
3   Insufficient contrast and lack of *strong accent*.
4   Monotonous tunes or the same one for different exercises. These faults do nothing to encourage the pupils to listen.
5   Sticking rigidly to the music, with no give and take in the speed to help the children. You should appreciate the little ones' difficulties and anticipate the need for adjusting speed and ends of phrases. When children of this age work individually, a different speed may be needed for each one.
6   Paying little attention to the class, so "missing the point" of the exercise.

This is a suitable place to say how necessary a musical education is to a dance teacher, who must understand and be able to read music, even if the standard of playing is elementary.

Exercises and progression

1   Hello toes and goodbye toes
Many teachers refer to the first stage of this exercise as "good toes and naughty toes." I prefer my method, as I feel the turn up is as important as the stretch, and tiny children will not understand why they are being asked to do something which is "naughty."

Sitting on the floor, legs straight out in front
(a)   Turn both feet up as far as possible, then stretch both feet.
(b)   One foot turned up, the other stretched, change over simultaneously.
(c)   As for (b) with arms raised, elbows into sides, both hands circling outwards.
(d)   As for (a) but stretch quickly in *one* count, turn up slowly count *two, three, four*.
(e)   As (c) but add head turn (right, front, left, front.) Feet change on each count, hands circle for two counts. Head one count to each movement.

Objects of exercise
(a)   Use of ankles, stretch and strengthen feet.

Hello toes, goodbye toes

(b)   Standing on one foot with the other pointed, steps such as spring points.
(c)   Slow *port de bras* with feet moving quickly.
(d)   Push off the floor for elevation and soft landing through the feet.
(e)   Coordination, sense of direction, disassociation of separate parts of the body, moving in different patterns at the same time.

2   Knee bends

A very important exercise, a necessity for all travelling and springing steps. I never advocate any turnout in the first stage of this exercise. Far better to keep toes and heels close together, in order to have knees bending over the toes. The fault of ankles rolling inwards must be *avoided*, rather than be allowed to happen, in the hope that it can be corrected later on.

(a)   In a large circle holding hands (usually with dolls between each child) feet together, toes pointing straight forward, swing arms forwards and backwards as knees bend and stretch.
(b)   Holding hands without dolls, heels together with slight turnout. Heels will remain on the floor (babies rarely raise heels so it need not be mentioned).
(c)   As (b) without holding hands. Use a musical introduction—two chords for children to hold dresses or, if boys, place hands on hips.
(d)   In second position, making a bridge over a river, ie standing feet apart over a ''band.''

(e)   In first position,—standing in a small circle or band, one knee bend then stretch feet as in 1(d)—spring.

Objects of exercise
(a)   Bending the knees over the toes, relaxation of knees. I call this "giving dolls a swing."
(b)   Knee bends without help of arm swing, some turnout without "rolling," emphasising ten toes on the floor, knees over toes, backs straight.
(c)   As for (a) and (b) with more control and use of balance. Learning to hear an introduction.
(d)   Even distribution of the weight when feet are apart.
(e)   Elevation.

3   Points to the front
(a)   Holding hands in a circle (usually with dolls) no turnout of legs, alternate feet pointing straight forward and close.
(b)   Still in a circle holding hands (a little turnout of legs) "bouncing" the foot in front. A light touch on the floor with the toes, like a balloon bouncing.
(c)   Walking with toe-first action, well-stretched feet.
(d)   Point in front, lift, keeping knee straight and foot stretched, point again and close back to first position. Very little turnout should be used.
(e)   "Bouncing" toes as in (b) but changing to the other foot every eight counts, with a spring; later every four counts.

Objects of exercise
(a)   Holding weight on one leg whilst moving the other forward, stretch foot and leg, closing working foot to supporting foot.
(b)   Action for spring points, feel of "pointing" without resting any weight on the foot.
(c)   Balletic walk.
(d)   Balance, slow rhythm, counting half time to the music.
(e)   Spring points.

4   Points to the side (*not* introduced to the *very* young babies)
(a)   With a partner, facing each other holding both hands. Point to the side and close in first position, using alternate feet. Partners should use the feet on the same side, ie one the right foot and partner the left foot.
(b)   In circle holding hands as (a).
(c)   As (b) but holding dresses or hands on hips.
(d)   As (c) but close at the back in the third position making the circle bigger.
(e)   As (d) but closing in front, starting in a large circle then reducing the size.

Objects of exercise
(a)   A feeling of moving the leg and foot to the side. Working with a partner.
(b)   As (a) with change of weight.
(c)   As (a) and (b) also balance.
(d)   Third position of feet. Moving the weight backwards the width of the foot.
(e)   As (d) in reverse.

5   Hand exercises—sitting on the floor

(a)   Big hands and little hands. Commence with both hands clenched. Spread both hands with palms facing forward on count *one*. Clench, turning fingers upwards on count *two*.
(b)   Counting on the fingers (as in mime) starting with hands clenched, raise one finger at a time, starting with first finger and ending with the little finger. Hold fingers down with thumb until the right count.
(c)   Hand circling, both hands simultaneously circling inwards or outwards from the wrists.
(d)   Meeting first and third fingers, alternately over and under the second fingers, palms downwards, try to keep thumbs relaxed. I give individual help to start with and children help their own hands by using one at a time with help from the spare hand. The middle finger (second finger) should keep well away from the other two.
(e)   Palms of hands facing, fingers pointing upwards, join wrists, then palms, finally fingers. Part hands in the same order (wrists, palms, fingers), leaving tips of middle fingers touching until the last moment. Pull away to sides keeping fingers relaxed and repeat.

Objects of exercise
(a)   Use of hands, feeling $\frac{2}{4}$ rhythm with strong accent. Preparing to bounce and catch a ball.
(b)   Clear, expressive hands. Counting to music.
(c)   Flexibility of wrists and coordination.
(d)   Balletic placing of the hands, and mobility of hands.
(e)   Hand and arm "waving," use of hands when lowering in "*port de bras.*"

Arm movements   taught with a "mime" background

To begin with, both arms should perform the same movement simultaneously.
(a)   Sideways action, use "wings" as fairies, birds or butterflies. I prefer the latter, it is a definite action (birds have many variations).
(b)   Using wings whilst running. Keeping the arms moving slowly and smoothly is essential practice when the feet are moving quickly.

(c)   A balletic " full *port de bras*" (both arms forward then raised above head line but remaining *in front* of the head). I call this "picture frames" giving the feeling that each child's face is a picture, looking *through* the frame, which must be in front of the picture. This idea can be carried forward into basic ballet technique: "For my part, I shall only say that I regard the arms which adorn the body, as a frame made for a picture" (Pierre Rameau, *The Dancing Master*).

(d)   Later (c) can be combined with skipping round the room or backwards across the room, for the same reason as (b).

Arm swings
(a)   First holding hands in a circle with dolls, give dolls a swing, bending and stretching the knees simultaneously with swing forward and again as arms swing back (see exercise 2a, page 28).
(b)   Opposition arm swing standing still. Tell children to brush hands on their skirts or trousers each time.
(c)   As (b) but combined with skipping. Do not bother about which arm is forward, this will come naturally in the end, if not at first, with 90 per cent of the children. Many little ones soon find the correct arm. Of course the back arm will need encouragement.

One arm at a time alternately
I teach by some definite action.
(a)   "Listening" to music, first with one hand, pushing the hair back from the ear, next time using the other hand. This movement is accompanied by a slight head incline towards the hand.
(b)   Pointing to imaginary objects, fish in a pond, aeroplanes overhead. Try to get the children to *look* in the same direction.
(c)   "Painting" using the hand as a brush (see musical exercises, page 41).

Head exercises   usually combined with other movements
(a)   In the first "grade" head turn also forward and backward bends are practiced as *"no"* and *"yes"* in answer to questions such as: "Is the sun shining?" "Are your dolls asleep?" This includes "pitch" in the "yes."
(b)   Head incline is started in mime for "listen" but in the second grade is practiced as a separate exercise sitting on the floor.

Chapter 7   Dance steps

Dance steps are universal. It is the style, rhythm, coordination and pattern that decides to which technique or nationalities they belong. Dame Ninette de Valois has told us how she enjoys watching national dance performances, noting the steps which also belong to the balletic vocabulary. Baby class steps can be found in many styles, eg galop forward will be "hop step ball change" in modern technique, "skip change of step" in Scottish dancing.

Skipping

The most obvious and natural of these steps is skipping. Though this *is* a natural movement many children cannot skip without help—even up to the age of six or seven, usually through the lack of ability to stand on one leg. My method of teaching the skip step is as follows:

(a)   First, I get the idea of lifting alternate legs (without spring), using "Jack and Jill" climbing up the hill, or "Wee Willie Winkie" climbing up the stairs.
(b)   Next "rides" ie holding both hands with child by one's side. Teacher walks with knees lifted, at the same time encouraging the pupil to hop each time. By gently directing the weight from one foot to the other one tries to avoid the common fault of always hopping on the same leg. I like to have the children on my right side, but if the child is left handed the best result may be obtained on the left side. Small children usually lift the right leg first if right handed and vice versa. (This can be noticed when they first begin to climb. upstairs.) In this way the weaker leg is always nearest to the teacher, who is able to give it extra help. This stage must be done individually.
(c)   As (b) but only holding one hand to aid balance.
(d)   Sitting clapping the skipping rhythm helps to "feel" the timing.
(e)   Skipping round the circle formed by other members of the class, who sit on the floor. Each child has a turn individually. This enables the pianist to play at the child's own speed, who is therefore able to be more or less in time. I also use this exercise for practice in sitting still whilst waiting their turn, and finding the same place again. Combined at times with calling the roll, so children have to listen for their name before getting up. Other times we go round the circle in order to have a totem effect. When pupils can do this successfully they are promoted to the second grade.

Once skipping has been mastered and the pupil "moved up," even if the step is not well done, I introduce it backwards, which is not natural. Humans tend to move unsteadily when not able to see where they are going. Starting backward movements before fear has been developed, eliminates trouble later

Learning to skip (a)

on. It is wise to do this one at a time, to prevent collisions, which could upset the class and put some children off trying again.

Skipping will be used in musical exercises, for runs, skips and walks, counting a given number and skipping the same number; and in the coordination of arms (see Arm movement (d) page 31). Ideal for making floor patterns, the skip step is also the basis of group dances such as "A-hunting We Will Go," which little ones enjoy and through which they practice pattern, spacing, working with a partner and patience.

Galop sideways—also called slip step

(a)   With the very young baby class, I place dolls on the floor, make a circle round them with hands joined (once this has been achieved) then "step close" sideways, first one way then the other, making sure no one kicks a doll. With a large class this may be difficult unless there is a "helper" on the opposite side from the teacher to hold the circle in shape.

(b)   In twos facing each other, holding both hands "step close" sideways straight up the room and back, without changing places.

(c)   As (b) with "bouncing" action.

(d)   Round the room in couples galop for *four*, stop, and keeping hands joined, change places with partner. Start again, travelling in the same direction but commence with the other foot. The pianist pauses after every four galops for the change of places. The pause gradually gets shorter as the class becomes more proficient, until it is done keeping the rhythm flowing. If possible have the turn to right, ready for the polka at a later date.

The galop forward I will deal with later as this is much more advanced.

Spring points   (These are not taught to the first grade)

The lead up to this step has been described in the feet and leg exercises (see pages 26–28).

After practicing the "bounces" with the toes and spring to change feet, each time reduce the number of bounces until spring points on alternate feet have been attempted. Each child has a turn individually with the teacher, or a student who might be helping the class. Facing the teacher, who stands with feet apart, the child is held by both hands a little distance away. The pupil's aim is to place the front foot in the middle of the teacher's feet. This system helps to maintain balance, encourages the point to be straight in front and keep the weight on the back foot. However a *warning*:

Some children are very heavy. This has nothing to do with their total weight in pounds but rather a lack of rhythm and natural spring. Therefore the teacher must be very careful and only help, never attempt to lift as this can result in injury to the helper.

Preparing for galop forward with head incline. The child second from left needs correcting

After the child attempts these without help, I place bands on the floor, "front doorsteps" we call them. Children stand behind the bands (keeping indoors), spring point alternate feet over the doorstep. This may be done over a line painted on the floor in a gym or hall which is marked out for some game such as badminton. But a band is better as this moves if feet are scraped along the floor on the change, or the child travels. The use of chalk marks I find impractical for the following reasons:

First, it is dusty and children may breathe it in.

Second, the marks rub off. If there happens to be a class in the studio immediately prior to the baby class there is no time to prepare these. In addition, the children's clothes may be soiled.

Third, some floors will not take chalk markings at all. Incidentally if the floor is left chalky the next class will suffer as well.

I take spring points travelling backwards. Often children, who will place weight on the front foot can correct this fault when moving backwards.

Spring points, or "spring pints" as one of my babies used to call them are very popular, very useful and very versatile.

Galop forward
I teach this after sitting down with legs straight in front, one leg crossed over the other so no space can be seen between the socks. This is an endeavour to prevent the "pigeon-toed" effect. Having placed the legs, the class count *four* to the music and then change legs. In the top set this is combined with head inclined over the front foot. It is also my way of teaching fifth position of feet and legs.

We now have the feel of crossing the legs close together, the galop forward is "walked" first before attempting the bounce. Always take this movement *across* the short side of the room, or if in a square room which is very large make some barrier so the distance to be travelled is small.

If a long space is available in front of the pupils they will race forward and never tuck the back foot in behind the leading foot.

Chapter 8   Musical exercises

The art and practise of listening is a very valuable accomplishment, which cannot be started too early. In dance classes for the very young this training must be linked with music, without which there can be no real dance.

"The dancer with no ear, like the madman, makes ill-combined steps, and is always astray in his execution. He continually runs after the time and never catches up with it. He hears nothing, everything is contrary to him; his dancing has neither logic nor expression, and the music which should direct his movements, order his steps and determine his temps, serves only to betray his incapabilities and imperfections" (Jean-George Noverre, *Lettres sur les Ballets et la Danse* letter 12, Stuttgart 1760).

First stage

I try to instil $\frac{2}{4}$ time (with strong accent) pitch and phrasing. Some of the exercises already mentioned are incorporated with these two musical expressions.

Clapping $\frac{2}{4}$ Sitting on the floor, clapping floor on *one* and over head on *two*. The noise made by clapping the floor is louder than that above head, giving the strong and weak beat. With this, I also use pitch by asking the pianist to play "down, up" very obviously (see Appendix).

Following this, I develop the "down" into rabbits and the "up" into butterflies, pupils changing when the pianist changes. I have also tried out a scheme of acting as "baby sitter" for their dolls, whilst the class did the work. Providing at least one child will cooperate and lead the class this works well and encourages the children to work on their own.

This same $\frac{2}{4}$ time comes in hand exercise (5a page 30).

Pitch   This has been mentioned above. I also take "going to bed and getting up." This is a gradual change of pitch, the pianist starting on low bass and reaching the highest note in a series of scales and/or arpeggios, after a short pause, returning to the original note. Children lie down for a rest, get up and stretch on the ascending music, then "go back to bed" on the descending passage.

This is quite difficult to do properly at this age, but they soon get the idea of the shape and change but always "arrive" too soon.

Phrasing   Much of this is introduced by the teacher "using" the phrase, stopping movements at the end as often as possible. However, I have one special exercise for this purpose.

Trains   Pupils are linked together, usually in threes or fours, one behind the other holding bands (train wheels). The "driver" leads the train with a passenger (or two), the "guard" looks after the train from the rear.

When music slows to a stop, the train must slow up and stop at the "station." Bands are used to make bridges under which trains must run. A helper is needed to hold one end of the band, but often a fixing for the other end can be found by using radiator knobs, window fasteners etc. This makes for better use of space. Trains is the only activity taken in the youngest class which is not repeated in the higher baby "grades."

Second stage

The developments of the $\frac{2}{4}$ and pitch exercises in the next class are as follows:
$\frac{3}{4}$ Clap the floor on *one*, in front of body on *two*, and over head on *three*. Remember to tell the class the extra count comes in the middle (as will be the case when they come to beating time—see Appendix). The "follow up" to this brings in *dolls*—walking with straight legs lifted in front and arms held in front at "middle" level.

Trains

Clapping $\frac{3}{4}$ time

Butterflies   are now linked with phrasing. "Fly" to the end of phrase then fold "wings" upwards (pianist waits until all wings are folded). Once again pitch has been introduced and appears again in arm exercise (c) (see page 31).

Skip, run and walk   is now taught both by clapping the rhythms and doing the steps to "Jack and Jill" tune played in $\frac{6}{8}$ rhythm or $\frac{4}{4}$ time played in crotchets or $\frac{2}{4}$ in quavers. Emphasising it is *rhythm* and not tune which rules the movement of the feet (see appendix for music).

Volume   has been used all through the classes, the accent being stressed, but *blowing up a balloon* is especially for this. Holding hands in a circle, close in as much as possible then "blow it up" as music becomes louder. When circle is as large as possible (without dropping hands), the pianist "lets the air out" and the circle gets smaller. This can be followed by blowing up balloon then "bouncing" ie keeping hands jumping with feet together.

Third stage

Add $\frac{4}{4}$ time to their repertoire. The extra count is added in the middle by a clap on the knees on count *two*.

Skip, run and walk   is now danced to a variety of different tunes and can be linked with *volume*. The class dance in a large circle round the room on the loud music, a small circle in the middle for quiet music. To begin this exercise always place some object in the middle to mark the centre for the quiet music.

Puddles and ponds   is a variety of the last exercise. To ensure they all understand a pond is bigger than a puddle, I make two circles of bands, one much larger than the other. The class change from one circle to the other as the volume varies, trying to keep to the skip, run or walk at the same time.

Tulips and daisies   Another pitch exercise, this time coupled with characterisation.

Tulips   start curled up on the floor (the bulb) grow up as tall as possible to a point, then open to a kind of U shape and sway slightly in the wind, then each petal falls off separately, leaving the stalk standing. It is very rare that babies manage to keep their feet and legs together for this, though they are often reminded (see Appendix).

Daisies (small wild ones)   begin the same way as tulips, but only grow up to a kneel (pianist stops "growing" about middle C), open to a flat flower face looking to the sky, close up at night and open again next day. Later I ask the children to listen while the pianist plays the "growing" music, then they say which flower they are going to be by the distance the pianist "grows".

Tulips and butterflies   The class is usually split into halves for this, one group being the tulips, the other butterflies. The pianist plays one note, either high or low. By this note the children should know which group is to have the first turn. Change the groups over before "guessing" again.

Speed   Variations in speed must be very marked eg Run and Walk which have already been practiced. In the third baby group we have "fairies" and "giants", the latter being the first effort with slow walking, for example one step to a minim. Nearly all young pupils find this difficult. We include facial expressions—fairies are always happy and smiling, giants very cross.

Clapping   This is now taken in the normal way (ie not on floor or knees etc). As a lead up to the common rhythm used in dancing of quick, quick, slow, two crotchets and a minim or quarter note, quarter note half note according to the method required, I teach three claps and open hands on the fourth count. The exercise is performed sitting on the floor. There is no point in tiring legs by attempting to stand up, the resulting fidgeting would tend to make this a waste of time. To encourage listening rather than copying, pupils may do this clapping with eyes closed. Conversely sometimes use the eyes to follow the hands, opening on *four* in a different direction each time.

Musical expression and tone quality   Using the hands as a paint brush (usually one at a time) raise the arm so the back of the hand is forward with fingers pointing downwards, then lower with palm to the front and fingers pointing upwards, in a hand-waving action. A $\frac{3}{4}$ time is most suitable, but not necessary. The pupils "paint" to the rhythm then we discuss what colour, the heavy bass being dark brown or black contrasted with a light bright tune in the treble for yellow, silver or white. Soft lyrical pieces become blue, pink etc. After some experience the children can say which colour has been played.

Chapter 9   Other class activities

The following have not been included in the previous text as generally they have no logical progressions, or because I only use the idea at one stage of baby work.

Bridge over the river   Place band beside each pupil (in a line representing the river). Step to side over the band (making the bridge) then lift the other foot over to point in front, repeat in the opposite direction. This can only be attempted in the top grade.

Bouncing balls   In the first class this is a break for a game, but has a serious side. The objects being first to encourage the children to join in (if this is needed). Next the use of eyes to watch the ball, thirdly, use of hands and arms in coordination with ball, also a $\frac{2}{4}$ rhythm and concentration. A great sense of achievement is felt when at last the ball has been caught. Most small children bend down to the floor to bounce, try to use only one hand, and often bounce on their own toe. I can think of many progressions for this activity, but never find time to include these.

A hunting we will go   When children can manage the galop in couples, I teach the casting off as elephants holding the tail of the one in front. Some children have seen these animals in a circus walking this way. The hardest part is to get the children to keep in order, wait for their partner and come through the arch together. A top grade activity.

Picking flowers   Has several possibilities—arm movements in any direction one at a time or together, eg picking a flower from the ground watching it throughout the arm movement, opening fingers to place flower in basket. Run to end of musical phrase, find another flower etc. *Might* be attempted in the middle grade.

Simple patterns   Holding right hands with a partner, skip round each other, stop, change hands and repeat in the opposite direction. Holding both hands with a partner, spring points, both starting with right foot. Top grade again.

In and out of the windows   Stand in a circle, either with or without holding hands. One child starts travelling round the circle, passing in front of its neighbour then behind the next child, then in front again. Continue in this way until back to place. Any travelling step may be used, but I usually stick to run, skip or walk. Every member has a turn. At first one must allow each pupil to complete the circle before letting the next one start. Later they can follow on in totem. Care is needed to keep the size of the circle, they usually close in (not advised until top grade, it entails standing still, not easy before this stage).

Follow the leader   is a form of group work. To encourage the use of space have a "home" from which to start and somewhere special to end.

Curtsey   Though very important, I make no effort to teach this before the top set. Before attempting a curtsey the class practise placing one foot at a time on the demi point (ball of foot). Stand with feet together, raise one heel at a time. Babies find this difficult. They take the whole foot off the floor and press on the ends of toes, or tense the foot and curl toes under. When the feet are placed more or less accurately, we slide the working foot behind the supporting leg, following this by a bend of the knees without lowering the back heel. Balance is a great problem.

Theory   is not mentioned, but by the time children leave baby class they should (a) have experienced all five positions of feet, (b) know the rules for knee bends, ie ten toes on the floor, knees over toes, backs straight and head erect, (c) remember the middle toe when pointing to the front and side, (d) know thumbs should be relaxed and eyes usually follow the hands.

Use of nursery rhythms

For the very young the tunes for these rhythms are good for the exercises, owing to their simplicity and familiarity. Many can be used for mime activities in the pre-primary class, but I have three favourites for use in baby class.

Hush a bye baby   (a)   Rocking a doll to sleep, whilst transferring the weight from foot to foot in second position, is the first movement (taken in the first class) we sing the rhyme as we rock. Any latecomers can join in without being embarrassed so this is often used to begin the lesson.
(b)   When step to the side and point in front (bridge over river) has been mastered, this step can be used to 'rock baby to sleep".
(c)   Lastly, in the top grade a little dance is taught, telling the story of "putting baby to bed", still using the nursery rhyme music, this is later danced to a lullaby. We play the rhyme three times doing one section of the dance to each verse as follows:
   "Rock to sleep, put baby in cot"—once through.
   "Pull the curtains, see if baby is asleep", say "no"—second time.
   Rock the cradle, look again, say "yes," creep out—third time.

Jack and Jill Already mentioned first in skipping notes (a) (see pages 33 & 39) and in musical exercise for run, skip and walk. To these is added the mime of winding the handle to pull the heavy pail up the well. Some imagination as to the colour of the pails. This could be done in pairs.

Dickery, dickery dock My first limbering exercise, sitting with feet out in front, keeping legs straight and feet together.

"Dickery, dickery dock"	Hands on knees, ankles then feet putting head on knees.
"Mouse ran up the clock"	Run fingers up legs and body to top of head sitting *up*.
"Clock struck one"	Hold sitting position, point one finger upwards.
"Mouse ran down"	"Run" fingers down to knees.
"Dickery, dickery dock"	Repeat first line.

Conclusion

In order to consolidate the few important points, several activities with similar emphasis are included in the same lesson, but all approached in a different way, with varying coordination. This is very necessary as tiny children cannot concentrate for long at a time, once bored, all goes to pieces.

Improvising will have to be done at times. Teachers soon learn to manage with less than ideal conditions, but varying ages and standards in the same class, dirty floors and no pianist, are three unsurmountable obstacles.

I have said technique is not a part of baby class, true, but remember to *avoid* injurious errors. Incorrect arm lines look bad but will rarely do any harm. Rolling ankles can have serious life long effects. If the ultimate aim is ballet, the turn-out must not be stressed in these classes.

The first class is the most difficult. The following is an example layout for two-and-a-half- to three-and-a-half-year-olds. However, with new children it is rarely possible to cover the whole class for the first few weeks.

Class table

1	Hush a bye baby	(Stand)
2	"Yes" and "no" with head	(Sit)
3	Walk to see pianist	(Stand)
4	Big hands and little hands	(Sit)
5	Bouncing balls	(Stand)
6	Going to sleep and waking up	(Lie and stand)

Hush a bye baby

7	Clap $\frac{2}{4}$	(Sit)
8	Rabbits and butterflies	(Crouch and Stand)
9	Hello toes and goodbye toes	(Sit)
10	Jack and Jill and rides	(Sit and Stand)
11	Swing dolls and toe points	(Stand)
12	Dickery, dickery dock	(Sit)
13	Trains	(Stand)
14	Say goodbye	

Numbers 2, 4, 5, 7, and 9 are $\frac{2}{4}$ time exercises; 2, 5, 6, 7 and 8 are pitch exercises; 1, 3, 9 and 11 are exercises for use of feet.

Exercises are varied so as not to overtire one part of the body. One must always be prepared to make instant changes according to circumstances.

Personally, I do not find an hour's lesson too long. This allows for a more relaxed approach and some chat, such as a message brought by one little girl—"Rebecca can't come today, she's ill, she's got—(pause) *concrete*" and the discussion about puddles and ponds with the little girl who insisted she *could* go into the water as *she* had rubber boots.

Teaching "babies" is most rewarding; we know "a teacher by her pupils will be taught." One thing taught by baby class is self control.

Part two

Pre-primary

*(four-and-a-half to five-and-a-half
years old approximately)*

Chapter 1 The link between baby and the first technical classes

Once pupils have left the baby class, teachers will obviously wish them to commence preparation for the particular dance style taught in their school. Mine therefore will be ballet, but perhaps some of the ideas could prove adaptable for other techniques.

Up to this stage the only aspect of technique has been negative ie trying to avoid faults and preventing bad habits being formed, such as rolling ankles, twisting hips, hollow backs and not listening to the music.

By the time this class is reached I expect certain advancement in basic movement skills, such as stretched feet on walks, skipping well on the balls of the feet with raised foot stretched, running in time with the music etc. As well as this improvement on baby class work I hope the children will:

1 Be more able to perform without the teacher dancing all the time.
2 Stand in lines.
3 Learn a few technical terms.
4 Memorise simple set exercises and sequences.
5 Practice exercises and movements aimed directly towards future technical problems.
6 Understand characterisations and "do" a lot more characters.
7 Make a start on musical interpretation.

This is often a difficult class as it coincides with the first year or two at school. The children may be tired and less well behaved than when they graduated from baby class. My experience is that this is only a passing phase.

Education through dance should continue. The general knowledge will have an extended vocabulary, eg in travelling round a space, whether linked together or individually, the class will learn the difference between *clockwise* and *anticlockwise*. If a clock with a seconds hand is not available a watch should not be difficult to find, to illustrate the point.

Opposition is sure to appear in some form or other. The meaning of the word will be taught in conjunction with arms and legs.

An understanding and feel for *shape* is developed by patterns on the floor, in the air and with the body. I often draw pin-men on the blackboard, to illustrate the bend and stretch technique of jumping and ask the children to make similar drawings at home.

Teaching young children forces teachers to call on their reserves of ideas and methods of approach. This also applies to training the less able pupils.

Chapter 2   Characterisation

The first form of mime taught to very young children will be characterisations. These have already been used by the baby class in conjunction with musical exercises. To continue this study I remind the children of the baby characters ie rabbit, doll, butterfly, tulip, daisy, giant and fairy, then ask pupils to think of other characters leaving me to guess what they are.

This usually produces lots of running about with arms flapping, the rest crawling about on hands and feet, or often hands and knees, neither group giving any real clue to their identity. It is a starting point from which to discuss what is meant by "characterisation", and give examples by the teacher demonstrating.

Those with arms flapping could be anything with wings, so I give examples of a bird, fairy and butterfly making the following points:

Bird   flies, hops or runs, pecks its food and folds its wings backwards.

Fairy   feet and legs move more like little girls, but they are never heard. They have wands and make magic like opening flowers or making people happy.

Butterflies   flit short distances, fold their wings upwards, "hover" moving wings with big "flaps" and are rarely seen walking.

Classes practice these examples before getting into further detail.

The class should be asked to find the ways of moving which apply to one character only. For example, study the following:

Lady birds   fly, crawl *and* roll on their backs.

Owls   turn their heads round so far they can almost see behind them, they spend time sitting "looking" by keeping very still except for their turn of head, then swoop on their prey.

Daffodils   Grow up to a tall point, bend over as they open and shrivel as they die.

Ducks   waddle on land, but move very smoothly on water.

Seagulls   can move their heads from side to side while flying, they "bank" like an aeroplane when turning, sit on the sea (moving up and down) to catch food.

Above: *left butterfly, centre tulip, right daisy*. Below: *rabbit*

Right: *Giants*

Chickens Body leans forward with head up, they walk with a jerky unfolding action and flutter wings without really flying.

Bees fly into flowers and come out backwards.

Walkie talkie dolls use the same arm as leg for walking.

Teddy bears are fat, stiff and do not have fingers.

Rabbits thump the ground with a hind foot, when frightened, to warn others of danger.

Although one tries to get ideas from the children, some help will be needed. Steer the class away from the impossible, like roses and lions. I do not favour

---

Suitable characterisations

Characters with wings	"Animals"	Inanimate
seagull	tortoise	candle
robin	caterpillar	puppet
penguin	cat	rag doll
duck	kangaroo	golliwog
chicken	rabbit	walkie talkie doll
owl	frog	teddy bear
fairy	puppy	clock
moth	seal	scarecrow
butterfly	crab	windmill
ladybird	snail	
bee		**Plants or trees**
heron		
	Characters from nature	tulip
	stream	daisy
Fictional	sea—tide coming in or out	daffodil
	leaf in autumn	willow tree
giants	lightning	poplar tree
witches		
Dalek		

Whichever characters are chosen general knowledge should be included.

"human" characterisations as these tend to become occupational mimes. Some children can be most convincing in extraordinary difficult characters such as snakes, elephants, birds in cages, hamsters, mice or fish. I once had a small candidate do a "record player" for her examination.

Many characterisations can be put into one scene such as:

(a)   Candle and moth.
(b)   Sea and seagull.
(c)   Ladybird, daisy, caterpillar, tortoise, poplar tree.

Once again the pianist plays a great part in the success of this section of the work in class, also during examinations, when these are used.

Chapter 3 Musical interpretation

If begun at a young age children can be encouraged to improvise, and, in most cases, enjoy this without feeling silly. Given the instruction to "dance to the music" most children will skip round the room. My advice is to start with the eyes and hands, then head and arms, in that order—hoping to develop sense of dance and feeling.

Once the movements have gained breadth, action by the legs and feet will be needed to make them travel. These will be less stereotyped if used to supplement the "dance" movement rather than to become the most important factor. I usually go through all the stages in one lesson, commencing after some hand exercise sitting on the floor.

(a) Make patterns in the air with arms, making sure pupils are reminded to follow hands with eyes.
(b) Instead of "set" patterns, ask class to find as many original patterns as possible.
(c) Make patterns bigger by moving the body. It will be necessary to place one hand on the floor when reaching sideways.
(d) Stand, so as to be able to reach further and enlarge the patterns.
(e) Move feet to make the movement "feel" better.
(f) Travel anywhere in the studio, keeping emphasis on the head, body and arms.

Encouragement is essential at this stage. For several classes no adverse criticism should be made, however weak the efforts. Gentle suggestions may be offered, but that is all if the children are to gain confidence and eventually enjoy improvisation. Great harm can be done by parents watching because the early results are often very funny and laughter is fatal. Keep the class moving together, there is safety in numbers at this stage. Try to develop a "start" and "finish." This I usually link with pitch. Listen to the music and say whether it starts up or down. Repeat the question with the final notes—this gives a "hook" on which pupils can hang a beginning and an ending.

Finding new positions produces very strange results, but the experiment is worth it.

The choice of music for interpretation should be neither a monotonous rhythm, such as an Irish or Scottish jig, nor too advanced like a movement from some concerto in a minor key. The ideal should be melodic with definite variety of pitch and rhythm.

Improvisation by the pianist is not suitable as this often varies when repeated.

Chapter 4   Technical exercises

Whatever dance style is chosen, ballet is the traditional discipline that trains the body and the brain, which can be the foundation for nearly any physical skill. Modern dance choreographers ask what standard of ballet has been reached when auditioning dancers for their company.

The balletic method is, after all, only a syllabus for examination, in the same way as piano pupils could enter grades organised by the Guildhall School, or for example, the Associated Board, and speech candidates could enter such tests under the auspices of the Associated Board or some organisation like LAMDA. Each university board has its own syllabus for GCE but no one assumes history is any different because of this. No one would say a professional performer played or acted in "RADA" or "Guildhall" method, likewise with ballet the essential fundamentals will be the same whatever the label.

Transfer of weight In pre-primary this would only be taken from first position to second and second to first.

(a) **M-arch** In twos standing side-by-side, facing opposite ways, fairly close, left side near to partner, holding hands.
1   Both children point the right foot to the side.
2   Place the heel down taking half the weight on to right foot. The joined hands will complete an M when feet are in first position, after the transfer the pattern will be an arch.
3   Re-point the right foot.
4   Close in first position. Drop hands, turn to face opposite direction, join right hands and repeat with left foot.

(b) **Hide and seek** In twos standing one behind the other. Front child stands still whilst the partner, who should be "hiding" to start with, executes the transfer of weight as in (a) thus being able to see over the front child's shoulder when feet are in second position. Repeat with the other foot before changing places.

Exercise (b) is much more difficult and could be impossible in a large class.
I rarely take *battement tendu à la seconde* as a separate exercise, but this movement has been included in the transfer of weight.

Demi plié Taken slower than in baby class, and now called *plié*. Most children do not keep their backs straight, one way of pointing this out to them

Transfer of weight – M–arch (facing the same way but the author prefers opposite directions)

is to stand back to back in twos holding hands. If they lean too far forward when they bend either they bump or pull each other over.

Grand battement devant has been attempted in baby class. Now the tempo is slower giving more feeling of balance. Still continue to take this in four counts so the *battement tendu devant* will be practiced at the same time. For fun sometimes we have a competition to see who can stand on one leg the longest.

    Only occasionally do I use a barre in the pre-primary class for the following reasons:

(a)   The teacher is not able to stand in front of the class when pupils face the barre.
(b)   Very often the children are too small to use even the lower barre with ease.

Transfer of weight – Hide and seek

(c)   Most important, at this stage they will "pull" and "hang" on the barre, which does nothing to help placing and balance, it just develops bad habits.

    I believe in finding one's balance and control in the centre, and often resort to the old-fashioned method of having a book on the head. I use light, soft books, "hats" we call them, for static exercises such as transfer of weight, *pliés* and *grand battement*.

Chapter 5   Port de bras

Port de bras is a *very* important part of dancing. The late David Blair used to remind us that "dancing is a science and an art." Without good *port de bras* the "art" is missing, expression lacking and communication almost nil. With *port de bras* I assume head, face and eyes will be included.

I still teach *port de bras* in the form of mime by the use of nursery rhythms, or little stories I make up as and when needed. As in all other sections it is important to adapt to the conditions—hot, cold, small class, large class, no pianist, generally good or bad standard etc, but some theory will be taught.

(a)   The numbers for first, second, third and *bras bas* (RAD Method).
(b)   Thumbs must *rest* inside the hands.
(c)   There should be the width of the face between the hands in *bras bas* and first, in order not to hide the face when going to fifth (picture frames— baby class page 31).
(d)   Always see the fingers in fifth and second position when head is erect and looking forward.
(e)   *Index* finger is always on top if the position has a *number* (this does not work for Cecchetti fifth *en bas*). Index will be a new word to add to the vocabulary and general knowledge.
(f)   In second position arms slope down like a coathanger.
(g)   Palms must face upwards in *bras bas*, as if holding a handful of 50p pieces.

Examples of nursery rhythms

(a)   *"Mary, Mary"*   Raise left arm forward to waist height and open to left diagonal.

       "Quite contrary"   Shake left forefinger three times.

       "How"   Both arms forward to waist height and open slightly (*demi-bras*).

       "Does your garden"   Kneel taking both hands to ground (*bras bas*).

       "Grow"   Stand taking arms to fifth (RAD).

       "With silver bells"   Open right arm to second (RAD).

       "And cockle shells"   Open left arm to second.

       "And pretty maids"   Circle face with back of right hand.

       "All in a row"   Step to right and curtsey.

I use left hand for "Mary, Mary" as children tend to be right handed, but "lady" as a gesture is too difficult with the left unless the pupil is left handed, then the whole movement can be reversed.

Names of arm positions vary in different methods. These are given in Part three, page 68.

In the following rhyme, the left hand is used again as it always requires more practice.

(b)

"Oh dear"	Open one arm to the side low (breath).
"What can the matter be"	Raise both arms in front and open slightly at waist height (*demi-bras*).
"Oh dear"	Repeat with other arm.
"What can the matter be"	As before.
"Oh dear"	As before but both arms (*demi-second*).
"What can the matter be"	As before.
"Johnny's so long at the fair"	Circle both arms down in front, to right side, over head to left diagonal.
"He promised to"	Lower right arm, left remains.
"Buy me"	Bend left elbow bringing hand to diaphragm.
"A basket of posies"	Count *one* ⎫ ⎧ With fingers as baby
"A garland of lilies"	Count *two* ⎬ ⎨ class (exercise 5(b)
"A garland of roses"	Count *three* ⎭ ⎩ page 30).
"He promised to"	As before.
"Buy me"	As before.
"A bunch of blue ribbons"	Both arms down in front and up to fifth (full *port de bras*).
"To tie up my bonny"	*"tie"* ribbon over head (mime for dance).
"Brown hair"	Open both arms, turning palms outwards (open fifth).

Simple story example

A fairy lives in a house (centre back of the studio), "flies" out in a figure-of-eight pattern, stops outside the front of house "listens" to the right, then raises right arm in front to diaphragm height, opens to the side (first position to second RAD) ending in a "point." Lowering arm, at the same time four galops to the right.

Find a little boy who is lost, "talk" for four counts, take his hand and galop back to the house.

Repeat arm gesture with left arm, say "yes" and wave goodbye before turning to go back into the house.

This is very simple theme, but introduces both arms working together, one at a time, some floor pattern, imagination, and may be practiced in pairs. This example is more effective with a pianist who can do expressive improvisation.

Chapter 6   Pirouettes

Any form of *adage* is beyond the scope of this age group. They are neither mentally nor physically stable enough to sustain movements or balance. The preparation for pirouettes is another matter, "twizzling round" is a natural pastime for small children.

(a)   *Cork in the bottle:* an exercise for "spotting". Stand with hands on hips, twist the cork (head) from side to side keeping the bottle (body) still. (The head turn was first practiced in baby class as "no"). Repeat several times. Next keep the "cork" still and turn the "bottle" from side to side the same number of times.

(b)   *Half turns across the room:* a series of steps to the side with alternate feet turning half on each step. This will need some individual help, especially to the left, but it has to be learned some time. It is a change from (a) above, and also prepares the way for turning steps such as the polka. I always encourage the class to look where they are going. Some children can use their heads in this way at quite an early age.

Chapter 7   Allegro

Jumps   taken in first position are very difficult, but fun can be had in class by working in pairs or groups.

(a)   In twos facing each other, holding both hands, taking turns to do the jumps. Count the number given, stop, and change over.
(b)   In threes, two holding both hands facing each other, the third jumps in the middle (like a lift going up and down) without touching either of the other two. The idea is to spring on the spot keeping body erect. By now we call these jumps *sautés*.

Hop (temps levé)   Must be preceded by a step to give impetus, but I prefer to concentrate on the "hop" in skips.

Galop step   forward is still taken in a straight line. When the time comes to dance this step round the room, both directions should be used. If only travelled in the anticlockwise direction, the step will be more correct with the left foot in front.

Sign posts   is a game we play for galops sideways. If I point to the right the class galops to the right and vice-versa. Remember when facing the class, teacher uses the right hand for class moving to the left etc. This needs concentration on the part of the class and quick transfer of weight.
    Galop sideways in a circle is danced holding hands, and used as a practice for knowing left and right foot.

Spring points   are developed by increasing the number of consecutive jumps on one leg (not more than four), before changing feet; also by dancing the step in patterns or with a partner. For example, facing each other holding both hands, both starting with the same foot.

Polka   The following two exercises I find helpful before attempting the step.

(a)   Step to side, right; close, left; step to side right, point left to side. Repeat alternate ways, trying to form the habit of leaving the working knee to the side.
(b)   Point one foot to the side then raise the foot and knee placing foot behind the calf of the supporting leg. This is difficult from a balance point of view, it needs to be practiced several times on each leg and takes time to find the correct placing. The normal child twists the foot round the leg in a bad sickle.

Holding the barre with both hands is advisable in this case.
(c)   These two exercises can be amalgamated, ie step, close, step, lift.

The Polka step is first taught from side to side in solo form, then in twos, usually each child will first have a turn with the teacher, or a student, before attempting the step with another child. Adults must remember to take small steps when partnering little ones, this is quite tiring on the legs.

Before moving up, pupils in the pre-primary class will have attempted the polka, turning with a reliable partner. The way has been paved in baby class by galops sideways in pairs turning every four steps.

Chapter 8　Coordination

Simple movements are joined up.

(a)　Two knee bends, point right to side and close, point left to side and close.

(b)　Point right to side and close, point left to side and close, followed by arms making picture frames once: are two examples.

Coordination of legs and arms will come in many activities but we have one game called "statues," in which we practice opposition, but any position or positions could be used. Class run, skip or walk according to the music. When the music stops pupils hold the given position, usually one foot pointed in front with arms in third position (RAD) in opposition to the feet.

Statues

Chapter 9   *Musical exercises*

Children in pre-primary still need to rest their legs at some time during the class. A pitch exercise can be given with class sitting. First ask the pianist to play the bottom note on the piano, then the top note, finally middle C. Get the children to point down, up or forward as the notes are repeated. Next tell the children to close their eyes and listen as they hear each note to "point to it", the pianist varies the order each time.

Another pitch exercise but one linked with phrasing is *"sewing cards"*. Pretending to hold a card, pass the needle down through a hole, let go of the needle, take from underneath and pull thread downwards; repeat in an upward direction. Pianist takes the music to the lowest notes in arpeggios then up to the highest notes. Each time the needle is passed up or down the thread will become shorter, so the musical phrase becomes an octave shorter each time until the thread has run out and the "phrase" only a few notes up or down from middle C. Remember to follow the needle with the eyes.

Not all the class is devoted to the "pre-primary" work. Some exercises from baby class are introduced so that the children continue with the familiar and enjoy work of a little easier standard. This is also necessary where pupils join this class without having worked through the "baby divisions". These children are at a definite disadvantage. I always feel a sense of satisfaction when the ex-babies shine.

There is need for "fun", but this must have a point. Work in pairs or small groups (even if very simple) can be more fun than solo exercises. An example of this is:

Car park gates   In threes, one child stands feet in first position, arms in second position (RAD) gates closed. Bring one arm to third position (opening one gate to let car in), "close" the gate, then open the other (to let a car out). The other two children are the "cars". Change over very frequently as it is arm aching for the "gate". Needs supervision, not suitable for too large a class.

Chapter 10   Class themes

At times I vary the class procedure by using the same theme throughout the lesson.

Most forms of exercises and steps can be worked in quite logically for instance, in the following exercises.

A visit to the seaside
Arrive on the promenade, point to the sea.
1   *Run or skip* on to the beach (find which by music).
2   Take off shoes (sitting) *one foot exercise.*
3   *Run or skip* to edge of sea (tide well out).
4   *Point lift point close* as they put toes in the water and find it cold.
5   *Springs in first position* jumping over the little waves.
6   *Walk* back up the beach and *eat ice cream* (mime).
7   Pick up spade and dig sand castle—strong $\frac{2}{4}$ time, dig down on *one*, throw sand *two*.
8   Pat sand quickly to make it firm (quavers). *Running rhythm* with hands.
9   Join hands and *Galop* round the castle.
10   Sitting, watch a kite flying, point up or down as kite swoops, by *following the music.*
11   *Run* back to the sea for the last paddle.
12   *Spring points* making a splash.
13   *Listen*—hear mother call, run back, put shoes on, walk back to the promenade.

Characterisations of sea and seagulls could be included if time allows.

Going to a party
1   Put on coat and pick up present (*mime*).
2   *Walk* to a friend's house.
3   Knock on the door, but first, *find how many counts in the music* to say how many knocks.
4   *Listen* for someone to open the door.
5   Say *yes* step back and *point* in front.
6   Step inside, wipe feet on the mat, give present and take off coat (mime).
7   Join in games "*A-hunting we will go.*"
8   Have tea, eat something with a spoon. Children take some time to get this. They often put fingers in their mouths and "swallow" the spoon, or never open their mouths (mime).
9   Play *statues.*

10 Sit for rest and sing *Dickery, dickery dock.*
11 Find a balloon and *blow it up.*
12 Bounce balloon *jumps.*
13 Guessing game (sitting) *point to top, bottom or middle note.*
14 *Dance to music or polka.*
15 *Walk* to host (teacher) *curtsey,* shake hands and say "goodbye".

Many other events can be treated in the same way, teachers will think of several particularly applicable to their own area. Very common ones would be such things as:

(a) Going shopping.
(b) A day at school.
(c) Picnic in the woods.

An ever-present problem with small children's classes is the limited vocabulary, the essentials of which need to be practiced each lesson. To take away the boredom of repetition, the plan must be interesting. The children should arrive in class wondering what they will do that week. Always try to include:

(a) Some basic exercises.
(b) Some basic steps.
(c) Musical exercises.
(d) Work with a partner or group.
(e) Mime.

There are many permutations of movements and exercises. Experience helps to prompt inventions and variations. "Stories", I usually make up as I go along, often following the lead of a request or happening during the lesson. For this the pianist must be in sympathy with the teacher and almost read her thoughts. When teacher and pianist have worked together for some time this type of relationship can develop.

If the suggestions in this book are of no interest to anyone else, at least they have enabled me to collect and tidy up rough scribbles used to help my students as aids to memory about what they have been told and experienced when helping with these very young classes. Also rewriting forced me to think more deeply about the subject.

Repeating a statement made in the introduction, these suggestions are intended as *ideas.* Each teacher should be able to put over her own inventions and schemes with more conviction than those acquired second hand from the written word.

Part three

Preparatory

Preparatory is the name I give the group of children who commence their dance training after starting school. They may be five-, six-, seven- or eight-year-olds, or even older. The basic facts must be taught first whatever the age, the presentation adapted to the age group. These pupils have missed the foundation provided in baby class. To allow beginners into an existing class, with no chance to assimilate the fundamentals slowly—as befits a beginner—is unkind to children already in the class, who should not go back to square one every time new entrants are admitted.

Though revision is not a bad thing, this can be overdone in a once-a-week class, to the detriment of progress and interest. The pace required for beginners would be boring for a more experienced class. Conversely the new intake would not be able to keep up with the class who have had some training. This could result in a lack of confidence, or complete disinterest and disillusionment in dancing for the newcomers.

It can be difficult to convince parents that their eight-year-old beginner will not be able to keep up with eight-year-olds who have been training since "babyhood". These parents find it impossible to imagine how much has been assimilated by tiny minds and bodies. There is only one way I know of dealing with this—that is for mother to watch class and see her offspring floundering.

Typical Conversation:
Mother: "I think Mary should give up ballet, she is not getting on very well. Jean is taking the examination but Mary is not so good."

Me: "I hope not, Jean has been learning since she was three. If Mary was as good, there would be something wrong with the school. It must be time I retired, and Jean's parents have been wasting their money."

Preparatory is a session of ten lessons, in which I try to cover all baby class work, and a bit more for the older members of the class. My experience tells me children make the most progress by starting at the bottom and working through each stage, only staying a short while in each class, until they reach their age group.

My first approach is through the music. The initial lesson only covers a small range of exercises, which I hope the pupils will remember (and practice) for the following week. My introductory talk to the "preparatory" class would sound something like this:

"The object of this class is to teach you as much as possible about the basic technique of dance, so that next term you will be able to join a class as near to your age group as possible. We have a lot to get through in ten lessons. I shall not tell you anything which is not *very important*, there's no time. I hope you will learn and remember everything studied in the first half of term, but if some of the younger members cannot master everything taught in the complete term, the fact that these have been attempted will help when the exercises or movements occur in future.

Will you hold hands in a circle, now drop hands and move out to the walls as far as you can.

The first parts of your body to train for dancing are your *ears*. Until you learn to listen, any subject may be hard to master, but in dancing the pupils must listen to their teacher *and* to the music.

First, I want you to walk round the room this way (indicate with arm) listening to and keeping with the music."

If the class is old enough, I use a "code of learning":

(a)   *Listen* to your teacher and the music.
(b)   *Obey* your teacher and the music.
(c)   *Remember* what you have been told or find out for yourself.
(d)   *Practice* carefully and accurately.
(e)   *Watch* when movements are demonstrated, when other members of the class are working and you are resting, also any other dancing available.
(f)   *Read* anything available, but find out what is true and reliable.
(g)   *Concentrate* in all lessons.

I usually take one of these headings each week and explain to the class that teachers can tell the pupils, show the work, help each individual, remind everyone, but in the end it *must* be the pupils who do the work themselves, if they wish to make progress and enjoy their dancing.

Having stated my intention of using much the same material as baby class, it seems only necessary to list these in the form of class tables, with notes of the instructions and explanations given with each.

For ease of explanation, arm positions are numbered according to recognised balletic designation firstly Royal Academy of Dancing method: secondly Cecchetti numbering: and lastly Imperial Society names.

Lesson 1

1   *Walk*   Round the studio, keeping to the outside, trying to keep time with the music, but no other detail.

   Run   Ask pianist to play twice as fast and "drag" out of the class what feet would do at this speed.

   Skip   Having stopped the music, ask the pianist to play one quick beat and one slow.

   Often the "dragging" process here is more difficult. In this exercise I try to establish two points:

(1)   The class must listen to the music.
(2)   They must do as they are told, first by obeying the rhythm of the music, secondly by doing as the teacher instructs.

This is usually a matter of continually reminding the children to keep the circle large and not crowd into one another.

2   Keep the circle, sitting with legs out straight facing the centre.

   $\frac{2}{4}$ *time*   I explain that music always has a "strong" beat, which must be counted *one*, but the number of beats in a bar can differ (Bars are rather like words in a sentence). This can be emphasised by the use of percussion instruments.

   Clap $\frac{2}{4}$ as in baby class (see page 37).

3   *Bath exercise*   This I ask pupils to practice each night in the bath. The warm water will help the movement. Remain sitting, legs straight, both feet turned up then stretched simultaneously. Having demonstrated, I usually go round to each child in class and press the feet up and down, so they "feel" the full range of movement (see baby class, page 26).

4   *Standing in lines*   I "place" my pupils in a set order with the tallest at the back, but if there are any under six years in the class I place these in the second row, making the sixes and sevens take the front places. My object in "set" places is for my own benefit, as all pupils are new to me and I get to know them quicker that way.

(a)   Stand with feet parallel, toes and heels touching.

   Knee bends   Baby class (see exercise 2(a), page 27).

   I now establish the fact that knees bend over toes and that when standing on both feet ten toes should be "on the floor," also that the exercise is to *stand* with knees bent, *not* sit down, keeping heels in contact with the floor.

(b)   Turn out *both legs* and repeat the knee bends. Remind the class the knees must still bend over the toes which together with heels must still have floor contact as in (a) above. Emphasise that *turnout comes from the hips*.

Standing feet together (as in 4(a) above). *Lift both arms first position* (fifth *en avant—en avant*) and lower. The feet are together, rather than in first position, because I do not expect beginners in their first lesson to concentrate on two things at the same time.

I tell the pupils all the following facts because a good position is not possible if any point is omitted. There is no advantage in aiming for less than perfection.

(1)   The back should be long with shoulders down.
(2)   Arms should slope downwards from the shoulders to elbows, wrists and fingers.
(3)   Dents in the inner elbows and the palms of hands must face the same direction.
(4)   Thumbs should be relaxed inside the hand; the space between the middle fingers of each hand should equal the width of the face.

6   *Sitting, head turn right and left* (see baby class exercise (a), page 31). This time I explain straight away it is really the *eyes* that should "look."
7   *Sitting, hands opening and closing* (see baby class exercise 5(a), page 30). Here I point out that *all* parts of the body must dance. Next I recap on all seven movements with reminder to practice the "bath" exercise.
The lesson ends with three limbering exercises—
(1)   Lying on backs looking at the ceiling with arms folded across chest, legs and body in straight line. Raise head and shoulders to look at feet and lie down again. Folded arms stops "cheating" by pressing on the floor and making the exercise a waste of time.
(2)   Lying as (1) above. Bend both knees, keeping feet on floor—stretch knees with toes pointing to the ceiling—bend knees again—slide feet out until legs are straight.
(3)   *Sitting up*, legs straight in front. Upward stretch with both arms— forward stretch (from the hips) over the legs and recover. This exercise I call *Capital L* using the idea of L for letter which is folded flat in order to place it in the envelope.

Before leaving, all pupils will shake hands with the teacher, at the same time reminding her of their names.

The first lesson never works out to be a full hour. Time is spent getting the class organised, asking parents to fill in names and particulars, also explanations re shoes, uniform etc.

I would rather teach a *few* very important basic facts and exercises, which can be assimilated by the average child.

If parents are allowed to watch, the interested ones will help the children before the next lesson.

Rhythm work with instruments

Progression through the term will follow the pattern of baby class, but there will be no time to include all variations of exercises. I "sit" my class when I can, to rest legs and avoid the habit of standing badly as much as possible.

I prefer short full skirts for girls, if necessary worn over leotards. The use of holding a skirt is good training to control the arms whilst concentrating on legs and feet.

Though I keep the children in the same places, lines are changed over by sending front line to the back several times and by occasionally altering the "front". This is important especially if the class is fairly large.

Lesson 2

1   *Walk* round room—toe first, trying to stretch the feet.
   Run on the balls of feet without "shuffling."
   Skip lift the raised leg in front with toe pointed down.
   Change from one to the other by following the music, also change direction, explaining about clockwise and anticlockwise.

2   $\frac{3}{4}$ *Time*   (see baby class, page 38).

3   *Feet exercise*   (see baby class exercise (b), page 26). *Make sure the knees remain level.* A general fault here is for the movement to be from the hip (this rarely happens in baby class). Ask the class to find out when this position is used, they do not associate turning up the feet with standing. The importance of the full turn-up for *demi plié* (knee bend) should be stressed and demonstrated. Pupils should realise in walking with stretched feet at the beginning of the class they have already made use of this exercise.

4   *Knee bends*   As in Lesson 1, but in $\frac{3}{4}$ time (slow waltz). Here I always ask the children how many beats to the bar in the music. My object being to make a point re *listening* to the music.

5   *Points to the side*   (see baby class exercise 4(c), page 28). Use second position of feet by name, explain the theory of transferring weight on to one leg before it is possible to move the other. Practicing this with alternate feet ensures the change of weight from two feet to one foot and from one foot to two feet. Children are told to aim for the middle toe on the floor when pointing to the side and listen for the "sliding" sound on each movement. *Both* knees must remain straight.

6   *The arm position is second* (*à la seconde*) obtained by placing the first position taught in Lesson 1, then opening both arms sideways, but only as far as possible without losing sight of the fingers when looking to the front. Arms should slope down like a coat hanger. Other details re palms of hands etc, remain as for first position.

7   *Sitting head incline* (see baby class exercise (b), page 31).

8   *Sitting counting fingers* (see baby class exercise 5(b), page 30). This would be followed by a recapitulation of the class with special reminders of the new points.

   Limbering and Goodbye would be as Lesson 1.

Lesson 3

1 *Run, skip and walk* In any order, but hold dresses to control arms; hands on hips for boys, and even girls if they persist in wearing leotards without skirts.

Reminders from Lesson 2 should be followed by the discovery that only at one time can both feet be stretched simultaneously (unless the dancer is sitting or lying on the floor) ie when in the air as in skips. I also add variations in volume, small circles or large (see baby class, page 40).

2 $\frac{4}{4}$ *time clapping* (see baby class, page 39). Also with eyes closed, to encourage use of ears or not copying, also this allows the teacher to obtain a more accurate estimate of rhythmic ability.

3 *Foot Exercise with hand circling* (see baby class exercise 3(c), page 26).

4 *Transfer of Weight* from first position to second position and second back to first.

To allow some degree of accuracy this is taken very slowly. First stand on one leg then point the other leg to the side, next place the pointed foot flat on the floor keeping both knees straight, moving the whole body so as one's nose is still over the middle of the feet. Return to the point, close on two feet, repeat to the other side. (Point wait, place foot down wait, point wait, close wait.)

5 *Third position of feet* Stand in first position, slip one heel into the front of the other instep, replace to first position, repeat with the other foot. I find this is the quickest way to obtain a more or less correct position, and the time factor is very important in this class. After explaining about closed and open positions of feet, I try to "draw out" of the class the fact that third position differs from first and second in that only one foot and half the other is visible and there are two ways of doing third position, ie with right or left foot in front, whereas first and second positions are always the same.

6 *Third* (fourth *en avant/bras croisé*) *position of arms* Place first position (fifth *en avant/en avant*) then open one arm only to the side. As a reminder for the Royal Academy numbering we say "one arm in first, one arm in second, one and two makes three."

7 *Knee bends in first* Not attempted in other positions until the placing is more secure.

8 *(Sitting) head turn and incline* Combined turn to right, look to front, incline to left, head erect. Repeat on the opposite side.

9 *Hand exercises* (see baby class exercise (d), page 30).

10 *Repeat* Only the work new this lesson.

11 *Limbering* As lesson one and two.

12 *Foot exercise for curtsey* (see baby class, page 43).

Organised "ballet" walk to shake hands and say "goodbye".

Lesson 4

1 *Walk, run and skip*   As Lesson 3, noting the responsibilities of working in a group, keeping space and direction from the dancer in front.

2 $\frac{2}{4}, \frac{3}{4},$ and $\frac{4}{4}$ clapping as the music dictates, also with eyes closed.

3 *Foot exercise*   With the hands and head (see baby class exercise (e), p. 26).

4 *Points to the front*   Fourth position of feet, slide straight out to the front, think of the middle toe aiming to the floor but *no* weight on the foot.

5 *Point to the side, close third position* at the back (see baby class exercise **4**(d), page 28).

6 *Fifth*   (Fifth *en haut/couronne*) position of arms. Place first position then raise both arms (keeping the same "shape") in front of the body line and where the fingers are still visible when looking straight forward, lower through second (*à la seconde*).

7   As Lesson 3.

8 *Head turn* to front right corner, look to front, turn to left corner, look to front. (Sitting on floor).

9 *Hand exercise* as Lesson 3, but continue the movement by opening both arms to the side.

10 Revise all new work.

   Limbering as Lesson 3.

   Curtsey foot exercise before goodbye.

Lesson 5

1   *As Lesson 4* (as a warm up) but using "Jack and Jill" or similar tune (see baby class, page 39).

2   Clap any beat in $\frac{4}{4}$ time. Class first count out loud, then clap whichever count is asked for. Later they clap whichever beat is indicated by the number of fingers I hold up. This is a concentration exercise. The class must be sitting where they can all see.

3   *Feet, hands and head*   *As Lesson* 4.

This is quite a difficult disassociation exercise which needs two weeks practice.

4   Still sitting *stretch both feet quickly* (one count) then turn up slowly (count *two, three, four*) (see baby class exercise (d), page 26).

5   *Knee bends*   Explanation regarding the importance of bending. Ask the class to try an experiment by moving round the room *without* bending the knees.

6   *Point in front, lift, point in front, close*   Rarely do the class keep heads up looking to the front, so we use light books on heads for "hats". This is fun and does produce better results.

7   *Point to side, close in front*   (see baby class exercise 4(e), page 28).

8   *Sitting, legs straight crossed* in fifth position (see baby class, page 36).

9   *Fourth crossed* (Attitude *Greque*) position of arms. Place first (fifth *en avant/en avant*) then raise one arm to fifth at the same time lower the other just a little. Return to first position and repeat on the other side. I leave this position until last as it entails one arm having further to travel and moving faster than the other.

10   *Hand and arm exercises*   As Lesson 4 with head turn to corner right and left on the openings.

11   *Springs in first position*   Combine knee bends and foot exercise (paragraph 4, Lesson 5) (see baby class exercise 2(e), page 28).

12   *Stepping to the side and close* in first holding hands in a circle, change direction at end of phrase (see baby class exercise (a), page 34).

Repeat any exercise *if* time permits.

Limbering   If any of the class can sit up on the first exercise *without cheating*, I allow them to do so.

In the last exercise there is a slight variation to help those who find the exercise difficult. Commence with knees bent, nose between knees holding toes of both feet with hands. Slide feet away until knees are flat on the floor, but keep hold of toes and keep nose between knees. Recover to starting position.

Teach Curtsey.

Lesson 6

1 *Walk*   Arms swing one forward and the other back.
   Run   Arms used as wings.
   Skip   Arms making full circle to each eight skips.
            Commence arms down. Halfway to first
               position *one*,
            first position *two*,   } coordination
            halfway to fifth position *three*,   and control
            fifth position *four*,   of arms
            halfway to second position *five*,
            second position *six*,
            halfway down *seven*,
            commencing position *eight*.

2 *Positions of feet*   Method and number of positions used according to the average age of class.

3 *Knee bends in first and second position.*

4 *Five positions of arm*   (I teach these as the Royal Academy Method, but this would be modified according to the style to be followed).

5 *Point lift point close*   As lesson 5.

6 *Bouncing toes in front*   then change feet with a spring (see baby class exercise 3(e), page 28).

7 $\frac{4}{4}$ *Time*   Sitting : Clap hands *one, two, three*, wait *four* (see baby class, page 40).

8 *Three walks, clap on fourth count*   This leads straight on from the clapping exercise 7.

9 *Pointing one foot with bent supporting knee*   Up to now both knees have been bent or both straight. Holding hands in a circle facing inwards. Point one foot forward, without putting weight on the toe, at the same time bend the supporting knee, close the foot as the supporting knee stretches, repeat with the other foot. Once pupils understand the exercise it can be taken holding hands facing outwards. In some cases better deportment is obtained this way.

10 *Sitting, legs in fifth position*   With head incline (see baby class, page 36).

11 *Head turn with sharp movement*   from side to side. First performed sitting down as this makes it easier not to turn the body.
   Then taken standing with hands on hips or shoulders. Next keep the head looking to the front and turn the body (see pre-primary, page 60).

12 *Galop sideways*   Hold hands in a circle first one direction, then change.

13 *Step to side, close* (in first or third position)   *Step to side*   Leave the working foot pointed to the side (see pre-primary, page 61).
   Limbering as Lesson 5 (see page 76).
   Walk to teacher—curtsey and shake hands.

Lesson 7

1 *Walking* Using floor patterns.

Running Introducing butterfly characterisation.

Skipping Backwards, eight skips to one circle of the arms, be very exact in coordination.

2–6 *As Lesson 6*, but spring point from foot to foot. In balletic five positions of arms I try to instil the rule that if the position has a number the *index* finger will always be the highest point (NB does not apply to fifth *en bas*).

7 *As Lesson 6*, but add patterns in the air, eyes must follow the hands.

8 *As Lesson 6*, but leave out the clap.

9 *As Lesson 6*.

10 *Galop* Exercise as Lesson 6 then stand and *walk* the galop forward.

11 *As Lesson 6*—Standing only.

12 *Galop step* sideways across the room.

13 *Jumps* from first position to second position, and back to first. This gives the children with tight tendons a chance to get their heels down in second.

14 *Polka exercise* (see Lesson 6, exercise 13, page 77).

Limbering and curtsey as usual but curtsey to the teacher then to the pianist.

Lessons 8, 9 and 10

These would follow the same pattern, but should be geared to the age and standard of the class. However, the following are items I like to include if possible. There is never a minute to lose in these classes.

It is not advisable to accept any new pupils after the second lesson, and if youngish children have to miss more than the odd class they often do a second term in preparatory.

Additional exercises

1   *Spring points* backwards, baby class.
2   *Polka step.*
3   *Run, skip and walk* varying speed, also with tambour, or clapping accompaniment instead of music.
4   *Step to side and point in front* first with straight knees, later bending the supporting knee.
5   *More characterisations.*
6   *Improvisation* to give a feeling of freedom and sense of dance—pre-primary.
7   *Theory*—Some further knowledge, eg some French terms.
8   *Musical exercises* for pitch, quality, "colour" and timing. All these can be selected from baby class, but will need a slightly older approach.
9   *Individual work.* Time must be found for each pupil to perform on his or her own.

Children need confidence and experience of "solo" work before joining a "regular class". They should not copy and must try not to "fade out". The teacher needs to watch each child to assess the standard for the following term.

Some teachers will, no doubt, be horrified at this "rigid" method for beginners. It should be borne in mind that this is a "crash course", to prepare children to take their place in a class, having missed the "baby stages".

I feel pupils must be given the basic material in any subject before being able to progress, understand or discover for themselves. Anything well done is more satisfying and enjoyable. Nothing will reach this standard if the foundation technique is not sound.

Basic progressions in the first five lessons

	Lesson 1	Lesson 2	Lesson 3	Lesson 4	Lesson 5
Run, skip, walk	In time to music	On balls of feet for run and skip. Stretched feet on walks. Clockwise and anticlockwise	Hold dress or hands on hips. Loud and soft volume. Stretch both feet on skips	Spacing for group work	Use of same melody for varying rhythms
Rhythm	$\frac{2}{4}$ time	$\frac{3}{4}$ time	$\frac{4}{4}$ time	Recognise $\frac{2}{4}$ $\frac{3}{4}$ or $\frac{4}{4}$ time	Clap any beat in $\frac{4}{4}$ time
Feet exercises	Both feet	Both feet in opposite direction	With hand circling	Plus head turn	Repeat Lesson 4
Positions of feet and arms	First position	Second position	Third position	Fourth position of feet, fifth position of arms	Fifth position of feet, fourth position of arms
Transfer of weight	—	Point feet to the side	Point to side, place down in second position	Point to side, close third at the back	Point to side close in front
Head	Head turn	Incline	Turn front incline upright	Head turn to corner only	Turn to corner with arms
Points to the front	—	Walking with stretched feet	—	Points to the front	Point lift

Conclusion

Having read the last few pages I hear such statements as: "Mary Smith didn't go through all that business when she started ballet, she went straight into Grade 2 and did very well."

Oh yes, I believe you. Mary Smith may have received honours for advanced work at sixteen, but she is talented—an exception to the rule.

I am dealing with average, just under and just over average children who will have one lesson a week as a part of their education. The careful all-round training of the amateur is vitally important to the professional dancer, and all connected with the production. Without an appreciative, understanding audience these pupils—including Mary Smith—would find employment even more difficult to come by.

Appendix 1   Examples of suitable musical improvisations

The following suggestions for musical improvisations are *examples* by which I hope to show the simplicity and strong emphasis necessary. It has been said "perhaps the children would benefit by listening to some good music, Mozart for example." I would never deny the fact, but this I feel is the job of the parents at home. No teacher would relish the idea of a class of twenty two-and-a-half- to four-year-olds "listening" to the classics, the age group cannot be expected to keep quiet or still, so the whole exercise would be a frustrating waste of time. In no way could such music be suitable for the repetitive pattern of baby exercises and movements. Class music is a part of the lesson and should be readily understood by the children.

"The gorgeous blue Persian feline reclined on the pale green hearth rug" is another way of saying "the cat sat on the mat". In the same way embellishments to the music will come later.

To train the tiny's ears all variations of speed, pitch, and volume must be exaggerated, there is no place for shades of grey in the very early stages.

I have proved over and over again through many years of teaching that this does lead to musically aware children with natural sense of rhythm.

Music used for exercises not purely or mainly interpretive should be melodic, lacking in complications but rich in variety of pitch. Children should be aware of the full range a piano can provide. Without giving any specific tunes, the following time signatures, with *approximate* metronome speeds, may be a guide to the requirements of the baby class.

Time	Exercise	Speed	Notes
$\frac{2}{4}$ time	Point close	♩ = 88	
	Bouncing balls	♩ = 32	
	Clapping $\frac{2}{4}$	𝅗𝅥 = 84	
$\frac{3}{4}$ time	Toes in and out	♩ = 98	
	Knee bends	♩ = 104	slow waltz
	Hello toes	♩ = 184	very quick waltz
	Clapping $\frac{3}{4}$	𝅗𝅥 = 104	
	Counting fingers	♩ = 104	one finger to a bar eight bars and a pause
$\frac{4}{4}$ time	Walking	♩ = 76	
	Big hands and little hands	♩ = 72	once to a bar (play in minims)
	Step close	♩ = 108	two to a bar
	Trains	♩ = 80	march

$^6_8$ time   Swinging dolls   ♩· = 66
               Rabbits   ♩· = 48
               Skipping   ♩· =104

Improvisation—Series of harmonised chords, giving no note values or time signatures, are available in some books of rhythmic exercise music. These give the foundation for improvisation and may be played as written, or, as single notes, in any time signature, rhythm, speed, pitch or expression.

Jack and Jill

Clapping **2/4** and **3/4**

Clapping $\frac{4}{4}$

Would follow the same pattern. As the number of beats increases the intervals in pitch decrease, so advancing the exercise.

Tulips

Appendix 2 Glossary of technical terms

Allegro	As in music meaning brisk and rapid. Allegro refers to fast steps of the balletic repertoire, often these are jumps.
Arm wave	A rippling action of the arm or arms, starting from the shoulder and ending at the finger tips.
Battement tendus	A basic ballet exercise in which one leg and foot is stretched in any direction, obtained by sliding the foot along the floor, not allowing the tip of the toes to be lifted. In this case to the side.
Bras bas	A balletic arm position (RAD method) in which both arms are held low in front of the body.
Breathe	A preparation, used in ballet classes, in which one or both arms are opened slightly to the side as the dancer breathes, and then returned to "bras bas" ready to begin a movement.
Cecchetti	A method of balletic training laid down by an Italian ballet master, Enrico Cecchetti (1850–1928).
Characterisation	Mimicking any moveable object—living or inanimate—by silent acting.
Demi-plié	Bending both knees over the toes without raising the heels (half bend).
Demi bras	A position of arms (RAD method), in which both arms are held forward, quite low, as though presenting a bouquet.
Disassociation	Mental control to move in different directions simultaneously.
Galop	A progressive step in any direction, entailing a step and close of the feet, danced with a little bounce, preceded by a hop.
Grand battement	A balletic exercise in which one straight leg is thrown into the air and brought back to a closed position. In this case to the front.
Head incline	Eyes looking forward with slight sideways tilt of the head.

Hop step, ball change, skip, change of step	A travelling step comprising one skip and one galop.
ISTD	Imperial Society of Teachers of Dancing.
Mime "dance"	The action of circling both hands overhead then opening into the shape of a Grecian lyre.
Opposition	Standing with one foot forward and the opposite arm in front. As would come naturally when walking.
Pirouette	A fast turn standing on one leg.
Port de bras	Carrying the arms through the air passing through given positions.
RAD	Royal Academy of Dancing.
Rolling	Standing with too much weight on the inner edges of the feet, so causing the ankles to fall in and weakening the arches of the feet.
Sauté	A jump.
Sickle	Curving the foot inwards when pointing instead of keeping it in a straight line with the leg.
Slip step	Step close sideways on the balls of feet with slight jump on the closing.
Spotting	Keeping the eyes facing front as long as possible during turning steps.
Spring points	A jump on one foot whilst pointing the other in front. May be danced continuously on one foot, or changing from foot to foot.
Temps levé	A hop.
Totem	In group work performing the same movement in succession, not simultaneously.